Valerie ©1978

This book belongs to

_____

Valerie Hubbard Damon

★   ★

GRINDLE LAMFOON
and the
PROCURNIOUS FLEEKERS

Grindle   Lamfoon

Grin' del   Lam foon'

and   the

Procurnious   Fleekers

Pro kur' nee us   Flee' kurs

Grindle Lamfoon
and the
Procurnious Fleekers

Valerie Hubbard Damon

Library of Congress Cataloging in Publication Data
(Library of Congress Catalog Number)

Damon, Valerie Hubbard

Grindle Lamfoon and the
Procurnious Fleekers.

Catalog Card Number 78-64526

Kansas City, Missouri: Star Publications

79Ø1   78Ø818
ISBN:0-932356-05-2 Trade Edition
ISBN:0-932356-06-0 Fleeker Edition

Published by

Star Publications
1211 West 60th Terrace
Kansas City, Missouri 64113

First Edition

In memory of Vertigo,
(my parakeet friend)

Grindle Lamfoon and the Procurnious Fleekers
is dedicated to all who made its creation
possible, especially the trees.

There once was an evening
so quiet and pleasing.
It appeared quite still,
    just as still as could be.
T'was not the case,
    for down at the base
    of a mellow,
    big Mellow Leaf Tree,
    was a curious sight
    concerning the plight
    of a tiny Procurnious Fleeker.
Now Procurnious Fleekers
    are funny bird creatures
    living in towns
    in shapely tall homes.
There are doctors and artists
    and nice teacher fleekers.
The cooks make the best goodies
    that you've ever known.
Now...
    Let's go to the place
    by the Mellow Tree base,
    where our story is now to begin...

It's dark and it's still
and there on a hill
    in a shadowy light so dim,
    one Procurnious Fleeker,
    downcast and befumed,
    mourns his poor plight
    by the light of the moon.
"Oh, Moon! Moon! Moon!
    so befumed I am doomed!"
    cried our Procurnious Fleeker,
    called Grindle Lamfoon.
"Tomorrow is May Day
    and all other Fleekers
    will have costumes with horns
    and marvelous bleekers
    and I will have nothing !!!
I'm poor and can't buy
    a costume with jingles
    and baubles and ties
    that will look so amusing
    with connections and fusings.
Oh !! ... Moon! Moon! Moon!
    I am doomed !!"

"Not so!" said the moon
	in a tune.
"What's that? Who are you?!!"
	said Grindle Lamfoon.
"Up here in the sky,
	a most obvious place
	for a face on the moon
	to be talking!"
"Talking?...hmmm..Talking!!"
Grindle sat gawking
	at the round
	smiling face in the sky.
"See what there is,"
	said the moon in a tune
	with a melody sweet
	and quite pleasing.
"See what there is??? Humph!!"
	Grindle flashed back a frown
	to that goon of a moon
	singing tunes!

"Stop teasing, stop teasing!
You're not at all pleasing.
I'm doomed and befumed
and you sing silly tunes!!"
"Be still," said the moon,
"and listen to me.
Listen .. be quiet ..
and soon you will see.
Now ...
look up above
and look down below
beside and behind.
Let your mind growww!"

Our Procurnious Fleeker,
   Grindle Lamfoon,
   looked behind, beside
   and up at the moon.
His eyes became larger,
   his face began smiling !!!
He rushed here and there,
   began piling and piling
   flowers and leaves
   and sticks and seeds!
Why, all around him
   lay marvelous beads
   and things that would bauble
   and jingle and bloom,
   such marvelous tweekers
   for Grindle Lamfoon!
"These things from the woods
   are much greater by far
   than expensive made costumes
   and Fleeker-made cars."

Grindle worked all the night
with flowers and blooms
    making bleekers and norns
    with gigantic plumes
    and all made of flowers,
    of leaves and of seeds.
The fusings were vines
    and marvelous weeds,
    free natural things
    from such obvious places.
Grindle had strung tiny seeds
    to make laces,
    and hung large bell flowers
    in the strangest of places.

His tarpers were threaded...
by dawn he was ready.
The bells and bafoonels
    were all holding steady.
Slowly and singing
    came Grindle Lamfoon,
    the Procurnious Fleeker
    inspired by the moon,
    up to the place
    by the Mellow Leaf Tree
    where all the town Fleekers
    came just to see...

the May Day Parade
of baubles and bleekers,
befits and bafoons,
pronurns and betweekers,
Procurnious Pie and Fleeker Popcorn,
red, yellow and pink procusganorns.
Oh, such a dazzling sight to behold!
Then all became quiet...
and up the hill strolled
Grindle Lamfoon,
the smallest of Fleekers,
with the largest and strangest
costume and bleekers.
Oh, it was truly a sight to behold,
to see little Grindle
acting so bold
and pulling his bloom-jingling
baubles and lorns
with pink and red fusings
and yellow-gold horns.
And right on the side
of the giant bafoon
was a hand-painted plaque
of the moon with a tune.

Procurnious Fleekers were
scurrying about,
singing and laughing
and giving great shouts
of praise and amazement
to Grindle Lamfoon
who sang *a great song*
like the moon with his tune.
The biggest blue ribbon
for the flobbeling lorns,
the loudest betweekers
and impressive ganorns
naturally went to Grindle Lamfoon,
the same little Fleeker
inspired by the moon.

Valerie ©1978

And Grindle remembers
to this very day...
the moon singing tunes
and what he had to say
of looking beside,
behind, and around,
by looking all over
there's lots to be found!
"See what there is,"
said the moon in a tune.
"What a wonderful song,"
thought Grindle Lamfoon.